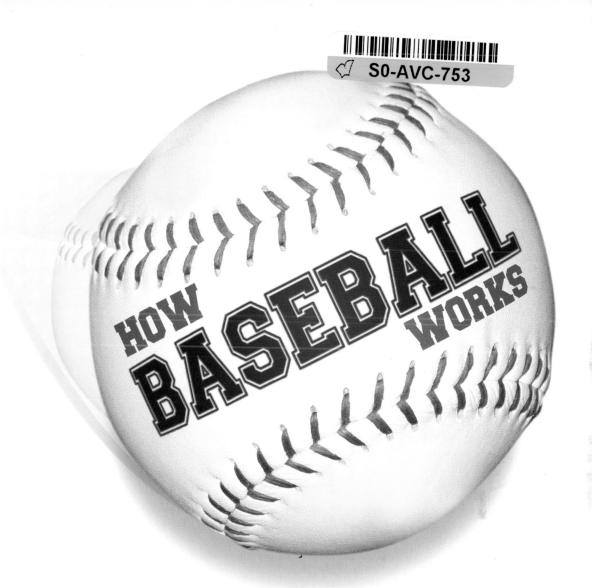

HOW BASEBALL WORKS

Keltie Thomas

Illustrations by Greg Hall

MAPLE
TREE
PRESS

Maple Tree Press Inc.
51 Front Street East, Suite 200, Toronto, Ontario M5E 1B3

Text © 2004, 2007 Keltie Thomas
Illustrations © 2004, 2007 Greg Hall

Distributed in Canada by Raincoast Books
9050 Shaughnessy Street, Vancouver, British Columbia V6P 6E5
Distributed in the United States by Publishers Group West
1700 Fourth Street, Berkeley, California 94710

We acknowledge the financial support of the Canada Council for the Arts, the Ontario Arts Council, the Government of Canada through the Book Publishing Industry Development Program (BPIDP), and the Government of Ontario through the Ontario Media Development Corporation's Book Initiative for our publishing activities.

ONTARIO ARTS COUNCIL
CONSEIL DES ARTS DE L'ONTARIO

Acknowledgments
Sincere thanks to all the super sluggers who helped bat this book home: all the absolutely fabulous people at Maple Tree Press, my patient editor Kat Mototsune, the ever-inspired designer and artist Greg Hall, the Baseball Hall of Fame, Russell Wolinsky, the Canadian Baseball Hall of Fame, Tom Valcke, Justine Siegal, the Women's Baseball League, Larry Dick, Craig Bodle at Source for Sports, Molly McKesson, Kathryn Massar, Jamie Calsyn, Dylan Kristy, Candice Mitchell, and, as always, P-J.

Cataloguing in Publication Data
Thomas, Keltie
How baseball works / Keltie Thomas ; illustrations by Greg Hall.—Rev. ed.
(How sports work)
Includes index.
ISBN 978-1-897349-20-5 (bound) ISBN 978-1-897349-21-2 (pbk.)
1. Baseball—Juvenile literature. I. Hall, Greg, 1963– II. Title.
GV867.5.T46 2008   j796.357   C2007-904041-1

Library of Congress Control Number: 2007938783

Design & Illustrations: Greg Hall   Photo Credits: see page 64

Printed in China   A B C D E F

Contents

HOW DOES BASEBALL WORK?

Fans, players, and inquiring minds everywhere want to know!

What makes baseball such a great game? Why is the ball so flighty? What makes bats perform so smashingly? Do pitchers really have the edge over batters? What are the tools of ignorance, and why is baseball such a mind game? Just how do players' stats add up? What makes major-league grass greener? Does a curveball really curve? How do pitchers get a grip…on the ball? How do hitters swing with such zing? How do pitchers and hitters work the count to psych each other out? And what exactly is the count, anyway?

Well, just like everything else on Earth, it all comes down to science (plus a few things science hasn't managed to explain yet!). And if you think that makes baseball sound boring, you'd better check what planet you're on. But, hey, why don't you turn the page and check out the world of baseball in action for yourself. It doesn't matter whether you play baseball, softball, T-ball, or even none at all. If you want answers to those burning questions, tips on becoming a better player, the scoop on inside information, or just to have a blast with the game, this book's for you.

The Year of the Bat

Crack! The tell-tale sound of a home run repeated over and over throughout 1998. Sluggers Sammy Sosa (above, left) and Mark McGwire (above, right) were smacking, whacking, and racking up long balls in the most explosive home-run race major-league baseball has ever seen.

At first there wasn't much of a race at all. McGwire had 29 homers at the end of May, while Sosa had just 13. But then Slammin' Sammy began closing in on Big Mac in a big way. He blasted 21 home runs in 30 days on a record-setting hitting streak. Soon the two sluggers were neck and neck, chasing Roger Maris's 37-year-old record of 61 home runs in a single season. Then, in the middle of August, Sammy belted out his 48th round-tripper, moving ahead of Big Mac for the first time. But not for long. Later that day, Big Mac hit two homers.

In September, in a game the sluggers played against each other, Big Mac smashed the record. Slammin' Sammy hugged Mark in celebration and Big Mac lifted him off his feet. But the race between them kept on. By the end of the season, Slammin' Sammy hit 66 home runs, and Big Mac sped past him, cranking out a record-setting 70. And fans everywhere were left wondering, "Just how do they do that?"

Chapter 1

THAT'S THE WAY THE BALL BOUNCES

Play ball!

It's the name of the game in baseball. Pitchers hurl and fire the ball. Hitters swing at it, drill it, and bunt it. Fielders chase it, lunge for it, and try to stop it from going over the fence. Then they fling it and sling it to throw runners out. Players even tag runners out with the ball. And fans leap and squirm in the stands when the ball heads their way, just for a chance to get their hands on it! The fact of the matter is, not much happens in baseball unless the ball is "in play." Whether it's alive (in play) or dead (out of play) the ball has a life of its own. The way it bounces, rolls, and flies depends not only on how players handle it, but what it's made of. Find out what puts the *oomph* in the little white sphere that rules the game.

Roll On In! ➤

What makes this smooth-sailing major-league character so flighty?

IT WEARS A LEATHER JACKET

The ball sports a thin white leather jacket that covers it completely—from round head to round toe. The cowhide covering helps the ball wear evenly, respond consistently to hits and throws, and maintain its shape. · · · · · · ·

IT STAYS IN SHAPE

The size and weight of a ball affect how it flies, so major leagues keep an eagle eye on its shape. The Official Baseball Rules say "the ball shall weigh not less than 5 nor more than 5-¼ oz" (141.75–148.83 g) and "measure no less than 9 nor more than 9-¼ inches" (22.86–23.5 cm) all around. And they mean it. The big leagues have each ball weighed and measured to make sure it's fit to play.

IT'S BOUNCY

To play in the big leagues, a ball must pass a bounce test. Random balls from each batch made are loaded into a cannon and fired—at 25 m (85 ft) per second—toward a wall made of the same wood that bats are made of. If the balls don't bounce back with about 50 percent of their original speed, they don't get in the game!

IT'S GOT STITCHES

The 216 red stitches that hold together the ball's leather jacket do more than just look cool. They help the ball fly through the air. Since the stitches stick out a bit, they disturb the air around the ball. This reduces air resistance, or drag, so the ball can fly farther. If a ball batted 120 m (400 ft) had no stitches, it would travel only 105 m (350 ft)—a pop fly instead of a home run! The stitches also give pitchers something to grip. By changing her grip on the stitches, a pitcher can vary how much, say, a curveball curves. Pitchers say a four-seam grip curves more than a two-seam grip!

IT'S PREPARED

Before each and every game, umpires "prepare" the ball. How? By smearing it with mud! But umps don't use just any old goop. They rub the ball down with Lena Blackburne's Baseball Rubbing Mud™, made from a secret recipe to be "smooth and creamy with a fine grit" and not to change the color of the ball. It removes a new ball's gloss and roughens up its surface just the right amount so pitchers can get a good grip on it.

IT DIES YOUNG • • • • • • • • •

The average major-league baseball lasts for about six pitches. Then it's toast. It's fouled away, blasted out of the park, or too dirty or scuffed up to remain in play. So the ump replaces it with a fresh, clean one.

IT'S UNDER WRAPS

The ball is officially signed, sealed, and delivered. Before each major-league game, the home team hands the umpire five dozen new balls sealed in packages signed by the league president. According to the Official Baseball Rules, the seals "shall not be broken until just before game time." So the ump has a chance to inspect the balls, making sure the home team hasn't tampered with them—the way teams did in the old days to get a winning edge.

A CHARACTER TO THE CORE

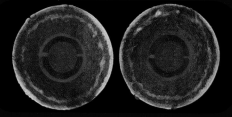

Here's how big-league balls are put together from the inside out. A cork core is wrapped in two rubber layers—one black, one red—to make the center, or pill. Machines then wind 300 m (328 yards) of wool and cotton tightly around the pill. Over that goes a coat of rubber cement. The ball is then covered with a jacket of two figure-eight-shaped pieces of cowhide, and hand-stitched with red thread. Finally, machines roll the ball for about 15 seconds to flatten the stitches. Checking the ball to make sure it's up to big-league standards (see "It Stays in Shape," page 8) includes inspecting the jacket for 17 kinds of defects, such as stretch marks and bug bites! If the ball passes muster, it gets the Major League seal. Then it takes the bounce test (see "It's Bouncy," page 8) to see if it's fit for play.

Ever since the first pitch hurtled toward the first batter, nothing has been batted about, picked apart, and just plain hit as much as the ball. Whether lively (bouncy) or dead (as responsive as the average caveman's skull), not all baseballs have been made equal. To check out its history, just follow the bouncing ball....

Early Days

Take a walnut or stone, wrap it in string, a cloth, or an old pair of socks, and you've got yourself a baseball! In the game's early days, balls are made from whatever's around, so the ball's size, weight, and bounciness are all over the map, er, field.

1845

The New York Knickerbockers and designer Alexander Cartwright (center of back row, above) write down the first official rules of the game. The ball's soft rubber core and small size (85 g/3 oz) make it really lively—scoring more than 100 runs in a game is a regular event.

1854

The Official Baseball Rules bump up the ball's weight and size. The bigger the ball, the less bouncy it is.

1860

Around this time, the first commercial baseballs hit the scene. But the ball remains anything but regular. Home teams supply a lively or dead ball (depending on the size of the rubber core) as part of game strategy!

BOSTON BASE-BALL CLUB.

1871

The National Association is formed, and professional baseball is underway (1889 opening game in Boston, above). A New York baseball manufacturer advertises that its "deadballs," made of yarn with no rubber, are the deadest balls around!

1872

The Official Baseball Rules call for the ball to be the same weight and size it is today (see "It Stays in Shape," page 8).

1876

Spalding Brothers Inc. starts making their "standard" ball, which becomes the National League's official baseball in 1878.

1901

Enter the Deadball Era! Lasting until 1920, this low-scoring period has players trying to get on the scoreboard by thumping base hits and stealing bases. Ty Cobb (see above) stole 765 bases from 1905 to 1919. Balls are left in play even after turning soft and mushy!

1910

Cork replaces the ball's rubber center and a livelier ball is in players' hands. But the Deadball Era continues, as pitchers keep scores low by delivering "freak" pitches—spitballs, shine balls, scuffballs—and by discoloring the ball so it's hard to see it leaving their hand.

1920

The big leagues outlaw the spitball and the scuffball. The death of Cleveland Indians shortstop Ray Chapman is blamed on his being beaned by a ball so dirty he couldn't see it to dodge the pitch. So the big leagues clean up the ball. Umpires have to replace marked or scratched balls with clean, fresh ones—ones that batters can hit more easily and farther.

1926

The ball's cork center is cushioned by two layers of rubber. The bounciness of the "rabbit balls"—even those used during World War II, which National and American League officials (see above) decided could be made with reclaimed cork and rubber—make home runs a regular rather than rare sight.

1950

Crack! Thwack! Crack! Throughout the 1950s, batters whack a whopping number of home runs. Everyone wonders if the ball is getting livelier. The number of home runs per game has been steadily increasing since the early 1900s.

1976

After a hundred years of making their standard ball, Spalding bows out and Rawlings Sporting Goods steps up to the plate. Managers and pitchers complain about Rawlings' "new" ball. But the big leagues insist the ball is exactly the same—Rawlings has made balls for Spalding several times over the years!

1987

Home runs are on the rise and, once again, people think the ball has been juiced up with more bouncing power. But scientific tests show that the ball is actually a smidgen *less* bouncy than in 1977. Hmmm...

2000

Home runs explode out of big-league parks like never before (see above) as the number of homers per game hits an all-time high of 2.34. The big leagues turn to scientists to test the 1999 ball and the 2000 ball, and find that the two balls look, feel, and bounce almost exactly the same.

Into the 21st Century

Another team of scientists has fans send in foul balls they've caught, and finds the cores of balls from 1995 and 2000 bounce on average .6 m (2 ft) higher than balls from 1963, 1970, and 1989. But they still can't say that the newer balls are livelier, because they don't know how aging affects the ball. They say more tests are needed to unravel the ball's woolly mysteries.

Quick Answers to Hard-Hitting Questions

Hey, what do you call the ball?

Over the years, the ball has been called a pill, a pea, a tomato, an apple, a horsehide, and even a pellet.

What happens if a ball explodes?

In 1974, a shortage of the horsehide that was used to cover baseballs spurred the big leagues to replace it with cowhide. The result? The ball exploded more often. *Ka-BANG!* Umps were instructed to use the biggest part of the core surviving the explosion to finish off plays.

HAVE WE GOT A BALL FOR YOU!

Funny things can happen when players and coaches get their hands on the ball. Over the years, they've come up with many special treatments to "improve" the ball's performance. Check out the sneaky science of doctoring the ball.

HOT BALLS, COLD BALLS, GET 'EM HERE!

Facing a team on a hot hitting streak? If you can't strike 'em out, freeze 'em out! Freezing the ball causes it to lose heat and, in turn, energy. It can't bounce as much, so batters can't hit it as far.

In the 1960s, a Baltimore Orioles coach froze one bunch of balls and heated another for a pre-game hitting contest with the New York Yankees. Yankees star slugger Mickey Mantle got nothing but frozen balls to swing at, and he hit pop-up after pop-up. But when Orioles power-hitter Gus Triandos got the hot balls to whack at, he slammed them right out of the park.

PLAIN DIRTY WORK

Since 1920, the Official Baseball Rules have called for a clean ball to be used. Before that time, players usually broke in a new ball by throwing it around the infield. This gave players a chance to rub the ball with dirt, squirt it with tobacco juice, and smear it with whatever gunk happened to be stashed in their pockets. Sometimes the ball got so filthy it looked black! A dirty ball is harder to see. And if a hitter has a tough time seeing the ball, chances are he'll swing and miss. Strike!

RECIPES FOR

Gourmet

The Official Baseball Rules strictly forbid any "discoloring or damaging the ball by rubbing it with soil, rosin, paraffin, licorice, sandpaper, emery paper or other foreign substance." Licorice and sandpaper?! Over the years, pitchers have come up with some unique—but illegal—handling techniques. Here's a menu of ball specials that have been served up from the mound. But don't ever try these at home—you could end up with more than indigestion!

Spitballs

Doctoring Ingredient: saliva, slippery elm (optional)

Method: Lick the ball or fingers (but not the thumb). The slipperiness helps release the ball so it spins very little. (Chewing a plant called slippery elm enhances the effect!)

Special Effect: Makes the ball break (move) sharply up, down, in, or out as it crosses the plate.

Vaseline® Balls

Doctoring Ingredient: petroleum jelly

Method: Hide a syringe filled with jelly in thumb of the glove, or stash a jelly-filled tube in your mouth. Smear on ball.

Special Effect: Variation of the spitball above.

Pitches

Scuffballs

Doctoring Tools: ring, belt buckle, bottle cap, emery board, or sandpaper—whatever can be snuck onto the mound

Method: Cut or scratch the ball's leather jacket in one spot.

Special Effect: Makes the ball break toward the scuff because the scuff disturbs the air, lowering the air pressure on that side of the ball.

Mud Balls

Doctoring Ingredients: dirt and water

Method: Stash mud behind the pitcher's mound. While "tying your laces" during the game, roll the ball in mud.

Special Effect: Makes it harder for batters to see the ball approach, and loads it with extra weight so it doesn't travel as far when hit.

Whitey Ford's Secret Recipe for Gunk Balls

Doctoring Ingredients: turpentine, baby oil, rosin

Method: Mix well and pour into a deodorant bottle. Rub onto body and uniform before game. Rub the ball on body or uniform before delivering the pitch.

Special Effect: Only Whitey Ford, a New York Yankee during the 1950s and 1960s, can say for sure. When teammate Yogi Berra borrowed Whitey's "deodorant," it glued his arms to his sides!

TRY THIS!

Just how much does the temperature of the ball affect its bounciness? Try this experiment and see.

YOU WILL NEED

- **two baseballs**
- **freezer**
- **oven mitts**
- **oven**

1 Put one ball in the freezer and one in the oven.

2 Get an adult to set the oven on low (150°F/66°C). Leave the balls for one hour.

3 Turn off oven. Put on oven mitts. Remove both balls.

4 Go outside. Drop the balls from waist height. What happens?

Which ball would you rather hit? Which ball would you rather pitch?

(Answer on page 64)

Too Sick to Lick

"Big Ed" Walsh, who pitched for the Chicago White Sox from 1904 to 1916, stood head and shoulders above the crowd. At 185 cm (6 ft, 1 in), and weighing almost 90 kg (200 pounds), he was nearly a giant back then. But his biggest claim to fame was a spitball that bedevilled hitters.

The spitball was legal then, and it was Big Ed's specialty. He could make it break four ways: in, out, up, or down. He'd look to the catcher, lick his fingers, wind up, and let 'er rip. The ball would drop—and slop!—past the batter. Big Ed may have been the greatest spitballer that ever lived. He does have the lowest career-earned run average—1.82—of any major-league hurler.

Finally in 1913, Connie Mack, manager of the Philadelphia A's, got fed up losing to Big Ed. The home team supplied the balls for the game, so when the White Sox came to town, Mack sent his ballboy to a stable to pick up a bucket of horse manure. And the sly manager dunked all the balls in the dung.

Poor Big Ed rubbed a manure-marinated ball in his hands, licked his fingers, and threw up on the spot. By the third inning, he had given up eight runs. Soon teams all over the league were serving up dung-coated balls to Big Ed. He lost his appetite for the spitball—and his winning edge. Maybe his arm had given out. Or maybe Big Ed had lost his stomach for the game because the ball made his fingers too sick to lick.

Chapter 2

THE TOOLS

Batter up!

Whether it's for digging into the batter's box, stealing bases, fielding double plays, pitching fireballers, or hammering home runs, baseball players need the right tools to get the job done. And not just any bat, mitt, or glove will do for a pro.

First off, every player's bat is different. Each pro has an individual model with the right shape, weight, and finish to make it a unique hitting tool. Some pros even use different models against different pitchers! Major-league bat makers keep the model numbers on file for each pro.

On the other "hand" are the gloves and mitts of precision that help pro fielders play each position. And catchers work with "tools of ignorance." Read on to find out what that means, and to get the inside scoop on the tools and uniforms that outfit the pros.

Gear Up! ➤

IT'S ALL IN THE BAT

Early batters wielded sticks and wagon spokes. Today pro baseball bats are still made of wood. What's more, they're made pretty much the same way they were more than a hundred years ago. And the wooden cudgel still performs simply smashingly. Check it out and see!

TIP

Wood? Aluminum? Fat barrel? Thin handle? What's the right bat for you? Don't sweat it, slugger, just swing it and see. If a bat swings easily and evenly, it's for you. If not, try a lighter "lumber." Pros say comfort is key for all players—Little League on up.

Knob

That knob has a real job. The knob flares out at the end of the bat to prevent the bat from slipping out of a player's hands.

Sweet Spot

The sweet spot—the best part of the bat to hit the ball with—can launch the ball farther than any other part of the bat. Even though the sweet spot is unique to every bat, it's usually found 15 to 20 cm (6–8 in) up along the barrel.

Barrel

Barrel away! The barrel, or fat part of the bat, is the prime hitting surface. The white ash the bat is made from can absorb the shock of a head-on collision with a 145-km/h (90-mph) fastball. In a split second, the wood bends out of shape, then snaps back in place to get the ball in the swing of things!

Handle

Hold the bat by the handle to get a grip on it—and the game! Some pros like to wrap the handle with tape for extra grip.

Quick Hit

See the guard on Barry Bonds' right elbow (page 17)? Some people say it should be banned because it takes away the batter's fear of one of the pitcher's best weapons—inside pitches that sweep close to the batter. But since these pitches sometimes hit batters on purpose, maybe Bonds simply wants to even up the odds.

HOW BASEBALL WORKS

"WOOD" THIS BAT MAKE THE BIG LEAGUES?

Major-league slugging tools are made from billetts, solid cylinders of wood, usually cut from white ash trees 40 to 80 years old. Bat makers age the billetts for two years, oven-dry them in kilns, and ship them to a factory where machine lathes cut and shape them. Then the bats are sanded and branded with the manufacturer's logo. The finishing touches: special wood stains or flame-roasting.

Superstar hitter Ted Williams (see page 36) was incredibly finicky about the wood that went into his bats. He'd often show up at the bat factory to personally pick it out. And record-setting home-run king Barry Bonds (shown here) is also picky about his bats' timber. Barry swings only maple lumber, which is harder than ash.

TRY THIS!

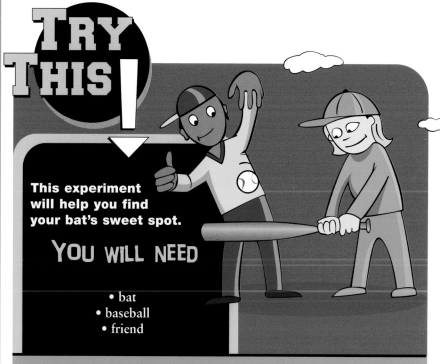

This experiment will help you find your bat's sweet spot.

YOU WILL NEED

- bat
- baseball
- friend

1 Grip your bat firmly with two hands on the handle, holding it parallel to the ground.

2 Have your friend drop the baseball onto different parts of the barrel and watch carefully. The part where the baseball bounces the highest is the sweet spot!

CORKING THE BAT

Fans wailed, "Say it isn't Sosa!" in 2003 when cork popped out of Sammy Sosa's bat. Even though it's against the rules, some pros drill holes in their bats and fill them with cork, thinking the lighter bats let them swing faster. But scientists maintain that corked bats don't give sluggers an advantage. Sosa said he mistakenly grabbed a bat he uses only in batting practice. When X-rayed by the league, none of the superstar slugger's other bats—even ones in the Baseball Hall of Fame—showed any sign of cork. Still, people couldn't help but wonder about Sosa's surge of homers over the years.

You don't need loads of gear for baseball. Grab a bat, ball, and glove, and you're set. But major-league uniforms and equipment have become an important part of the game. In 1849, the New York Knickerbockers strolled onto the field in the first official uniform: blue wool trousers, webbed belts, white shirts, and straw hats (see page 10). Since then, baseball gear has evolved to protect players and help them make the most out of every move.

1 Cap

By 1876, baseball's chaps had pitched out straw hats in favor of caps to keep the sun's heat off their heads and shield their eyes from its light. Pros look for a snug fit, so their caps don't slip down and block their view of the action.

2 Shirt

- According to an 1898 baseball equipment catalog, major-league uniforms were made from "all wool eight ounce athletic flannel." Shirts came with laced, buttoned, or shielded fronts.
- In 1929, the New York Yankees were one of the first teams to put numbers on their jerseys. A player's number was his spot in the batting order.
- Today, big-league players wear traditional button-down jerseys along with under-shirts. Some batters also wear padded vests for extra protection from the ball.

3 Pants

Pros have a choice: long pants or knee-length pants. Some players wear pads under their pants for extra protection when they hit the ground to slide into bases.

4 Stirrups & Socks

Players wear sweat socks; some uniforms include stirrups to wear over them.

5 Shoes

Major leaguers wear running shoes with metal spikes on natural grass, or rubber cleats on artificial turf. Spikes and cleats help them get maximum traction in the batter's box and base paths.

Quick Hit

A protective cup held in place by an athletic supporter, or jock strap, is essential for guys in the big leagues, Little League, and all leagues in between.

Batting Helmet

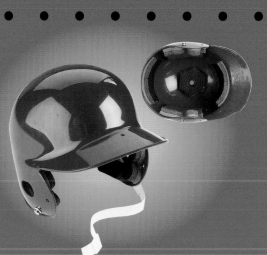

Hitters and base runners wear batting helmets with a strong plastic shell. Ear flaps and foam inserts shield their brainy craniums from wild pitches and throws.

Gloves and Mitts

All pro gloves and mitts are made of leather. Some fielders like gloves with open webbing so they can see the ball while they're catching. Pitchers like closed webbing to hide their grip on the ball, so batters can't tell what pitch they're about to dish up. But pitchers' gloves can't be white or gray, because then it would be too tough for batters to see the release of the ball.

HANDS OF TIME

Early days Bare hands rule all corners of the baseball diamond.

1869 Doug Allison, catcher for the Cincinnati Red Stockings, wears a leather mitt he had made by a saddlemaker. But it doesn't catch on.

1875 The first glove creeps onto the field on the hand of Charles Waitt. It's thin and flesh-colored, but players and fans notice the glove and call Charles a "sissy"!

Late 1870s More and more players decide that gloves aren't just for sissies. They wear fingerless gloves with padding on the palms for protection from bruises, fractured bones, and swollen fingers.

1880s Pitchers get the green light to throw overhand pitches, which pack more of a wallop. Catchers slip full-fingered padded gloves on their catching hand, and a tighter fingerless glove on their throwing hand.

1888 Buck Ewing, catcher for the New York Giants, perches behind home plate wearing a pillow-type mitt much like a modern-day catcher's mitt.

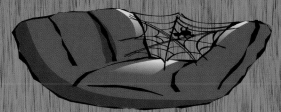

1920 Spitball pitcher Bill Doak of the St. Louis Cardinals thinks gloves can do more than provide protection—they can help players catch the ball. He proves it by designing a glove with a web between the first finger and thumb—a built-in pocket for the ball!

1925 A three-fingered glove for fielders hits the game.

1941 Equipment manufacturers bring out the Trapper—a glove with a deep pocket. It catches on with first basemen and gets called the Claw.

1948 Five-fingered gloves give fielders more control over the pocket.

Into the 21st Century Modern gloves are bigger, more comfortable, and more padded than ever. Some feature high-tech designs that can help stop the ball from spinning once it lands in the glove. Talk about making a sure catch!

Major-league players have a few select tools beyond the basic bat, ball, and uniform.

TOOLS TO GET A GRIP

Some batters wear batting gloves like the ones shown above—on both hands or just the bottom one—for extra grip on their bats. Others like to get down and dirty with their bare hands, smearing gluey pine tar on their bat handles.

Sitting behind the mound (see right) is the tool pitchers use to get a better grip on the ball—a rosin bag. Dusting dry rosin powder from this cloth bag over the throwing hand makes a pitcher's fingers just sticky enough for control. But dusting the powder over the ball is strictly forbidden.

TOOLS OF IGNORANCE

Why is the catcher's gear called the tools of ignorance? Call it ignorance, but we don't know! Maybe people think that, to put themselves in the direct line of fire of more than 100 blistering pitches every game, catchers have to be crazy or just plain stupid. Between getting clubbed by the bat and holding the pitcher's target— their mitt—right in their hands, catchers need all the protective tools they can get (see right): a mask, a helmet, a neck protector, a throat guard, a chest protector, shin guards, and a larger than normal glove with extra padding.

Hey—maybe all those protective devices should be called smart tools. Not only do they provide protection, but they are usually worn by one of the smartest players on the team. How many other players know just how to handle pitchers on the mound or what pitches to call to strike out the opposition?

Quick Hit

Is bubble gum essential big-league equipment? Equipment managers pack it for the road and many players chew it. In 2002, two wads chewed by outfielder Luis Gonzalez fetched a cool $10,000 in an auction. Now that's dough to blow!

Girls
GO TO BAT

When girls and women took the field in the 1870s, they did it with style and skill. They wore high-necked, frilly blouses, long skirts with underskirts, and high button shoes—a good 15 kg (30 pounds) of "uniform" that made basic maneuvering no easy job. But in the 1890s, Amelia Bloomer cut a long skirt down the middle and sewed it into a pair of loose-fitting pants. These "bloomers" gave women more freedom to move, and teams of Bloomer Girls bloomed all over America. From the 1890s till 1934, the Bloomer Girls (see right) criss-crossed the country, challenging local, semi-pro, and minor-league men's teams to diamond duels. Go grrls!

Quick
Answers to
Hard-Hitting
Questions

Why are teams called white sox and red sox?

When the National League was born in the late 1800s, it was the color of the socks that identified the teams. Chicago White Sox players wore caps of different colors, but they all wore white socks. Eventually, each ball club began wearing socks of a particular hue: Boston wore red socks, Buffalo gray, Worcester blue, Detroit gold, and New York green.

Do players do their own laundry?

Fat chance! Big-league teams have an equipment manager to make sure all the uniforms are freshly laundered, mended, and hung up in the dressing room, waiting for players to arrive. The equipment manager is also in charge of all the other equipment—bats, helmets, jackets, sunglasses, gum, pine tar, shoelaces. When the team goes on the road, he packs it all up then unpacks it on the other end.

How Baseball Got a Hockey Mask

Whack! A foul ball struck Toronto Blue Jays catcher Charlie O'Brien square in the mask. Charlie scrambled to catch it, even though he felt like he'd been punched in the face. The batter fouled the next pitch, too, and—whack!—the ball smacked Charlie in the mask again. When he came up with the ball once more, Charlie was "seeing stars." Looking back, he can't even remember which game it was!

Then at a hockey game, Charlie noticed that when the puck smashed goalies in the noggin, they barely missed a beat. During spring training 1996, a friend who played hockey for the Tampa Bay Lightning let Charlie try on a goalie mask. Then and there, Charlie decided he wanted something like it.

So he got to work with a company that made goalie masks. They designed a goalie-like mask for catchers with a built-in helmet. The new mask gave Charlie more protection than the traditional wire mask and cap combination. It deflected balls and bats better, and provided more shock absorption and a better view of the action. Charlie started wearing it in the 1996 season. And the "hockey mask" soon caught on with major league, minor league, and Little League catchers everywhere.

Chapter 3

THE COMPLETE ATHLETE

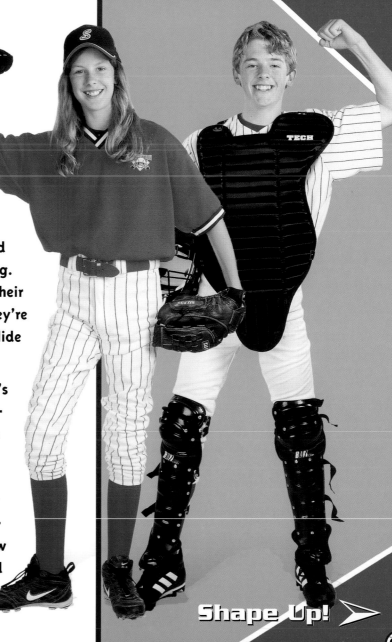

Whhhhhft! They swing with enormous power, throw with lightning speed, and sprint like the wind. Pro baseball players are bigger, stronger, and faster than ever before. What's their secret? Training, training, and more training!

Gone are the days when players showed up in rusty condition for spring training. Top players train year-round to keep their bodies in tip-top playing condition. If they're not in great playing shape, they might slide back to the minors.

There's only one way to keep baseball's "five tools"—hitting, power-hitting, running, fielding, and throwing—well-oiled and ready to go at the drop of a hat, er, bat. Practice, practice, practice! Players also train their minds. In fact, experts say the mind is one of baseball's most important tools. Get the inside story on how today's pros sharpen the physical and mental tools of the game.

P ssssst—ever heard the old saying "baseball players are made not born"? Pros train and practice till they can practically throw and swing in their sleep. Check out their workout tricks and toys.

TRAIN AND YOU WILL GAIN

J ust how do pros condition their bodies into first-rate shape? They work out to develop strength, power, balance, coordination, flexibility, quick reaction times, and endurance (the ability to go all out without letting up).

Major leaguers always warm up by jogging, cycling, skipping rope, or the like. Warm muscles are less likely to tear and put a player on the injured list. Stretching out the muscles also helps develop the flexibility to stop and start suddenly during games, and to lunge after the ball without falling to pieces.

Many pros pump iron, or lift weights, to develop their muscles' strength and power. But they're not trying to bulk up like the Incredible Hulk! Massive

muscles may cut down the range of motion players need to swing the bat and throw the ball.

Sprinting around the baseball field develops speed for baserunning. And running long distances increases a player's endurance.

A workout might include medicine balls—rubber balls weighing from 1 to 7 kg (2–16 pounds). Players toss, push, jump, and lunge with medicine balls to build strength in the body's core— abdomen, back, hips, and upper legs. Strengthening the core helps pros develop balance and explosive rotational power to hit or pitch the ball. Pros also do plyometrics—jumping and bounding exercises with a box—to build leg muscles that can react quickly and powerfully on the field (see above left).

Some players even stand on balancing toys—like skateboards without wheels set on balls—and hurl Nerfballs at each other. Why? It helps develop balance, coordination, and control for plays they have to make in the air, and speeds up their reaction times. Pros do what it takes to get in champion playing shape.

What's the drill?

Drills are set ways to practice that players use to improve their moves. Players practice how they want to play. Drills simulate, or act out, game situations, and they make sure the player is practicing each move correctly. Practicing good techniques over and over makes them automatic for real games when things are really on the line.

What makes up a good diet to play on?

Baseball players need to fuel up on a variety of foods that supply carbohydrates, fats, and proteins in the following "pro-portions:"

- 55% carbohydrates: breads, cereals, pasta, fruit, and vegetables give ball players their #1 source of energy.
- 25% proteins: chicken, beef, fish, milk, eggs, nuts, and soy help players' bodies maintain muscle mass and repair tissue.
- 20% fats: cheese, yogurt, peanut butter, and salad oil give and store energy for players.

FUEL UP

You can't run, hit, pitch, or catch on empty. Your body needs fuel—food—in the tank. But that doesn't mean you should eat like there's no tomorrow. Lugging extra weight around will slow you down, make you less agile, and keep you from going all out.

Top players fuel up to be in the best playing shape they can. Super slugger Barry Bonds even has personal nutritionists and chefs! Many major leaguers don't like to fill 'er up with a big meal just before a game, but prefer to compete on an empty stomach for settled nerves. So they eat well-balanced diets well ahead of game day, combining carbs to provide energy, proteins to maintain muscle mass and repair tissue, and fats to store energy for when they need it. This routine makes sense because, when muscles swing into action, they mainly use stored fuel from previous meals.

TIP

It's not safe for Little Leaguers to pump iron, but you can build up great muscle memory by learning and practicing to bat, throw, and catch correctly. What's more, you can cross-train by playing other sports you love. Experts say playing a variety of sports is good for growing bodies. But whatever you do, the #1 thing is to have fun!

Quick Hit

The San Francisco Giants once did a study that revealed it takes at least 10,000 hours of practice for a player to become major-league material. And that's not including game time!

STAR

The weight of Babe Ruth, a superstar in the 1920s, often ballooned from 95 kg (210 pounds) to 125 kg (275 pounds). Ruth's game day breakfast was a huge steak, fried potatoes, six fried eggs, a pot of coffee, and a liter (quart) of whisky with ginger ale!

Babe Ruth

GRRL CRASHES GUYS' LITTLE LEAGUE

Experts say ball players must be aggressive—bold or daring—to win. In 1950, 12-year-old Kathryn Johnston (now Kathryn Massar) wanted to try out for Little League, where no girl had ever played before. She hid her hair under a baseball cap, took the name "Tubby" from a comic book, and made the team. Tubby played first base for a few weeks—

then told the coach she was a girl. But the coach and team didn't care, because she had proved she was one of the best players there. Kathryn says that she had always been a little aggressive: "There was one time someone was running around first base and I tripped him. And then, when I slid into home plate, I knocked the catcher over." *Crash!*

Slam! A baserunner and second baseman crash into each other at second base. Whomp! A pitch strikes a batter in the arm. Players sure take their lumps and bumps in baseball. But advances in sports medicine and training are helping pro baseball players recover and get back in the game faster. Some even try to stop injuries before they start!

THE ELBOW FIX

Elbow injuries once sidelined more pitchers than big-league owners and managers liked to think about. The human elbow is not designed to take the wear and tear of pitching. Throwing overhand pitches puts incredible stress on the joint. Repeated throws can eventually tear the ligaments, or connective tissue, that attach the forearm bones to the upper arm bone in the elbow joint. *Snap!* goes a ligament and pitchers may feel a *pop* as their arm unexpectedly springs back. Ouch!

In the old days, there was no treatment for a blown-out elbow. But that changed in 1974, when pitcher Tommy John (see left) underwent a radical procedure that gave his elbow a second pitching life.

As surgeon Frank Jobe was operating on Tommy's elbow, he discovered that the ligament was so shredded it looked like spaghetti. He couldn't fix the damage, and figured the only way Tommy would have a chance to pitch again was with a new ligament. So he removed a tendon from Tommy's forearm and attached it to the elbow in place of the damaged ligament.

At the time, doctors told Tommy his chances of pitching again in the major leagues were 1 in 100. But Tommy gave it a shot. He worked to recondition his arm. Eighteen months and another operation later, he was back on the mound. The brave pitcher threw in the major leagues for another 14 years and won more games than ever before.

Since then, "Tommy John" surgery has become a routine operation that many pitchers undergo to rebuild elbows—sometimes more than once! Over the years, improvements in technique and rehabilitation, or recovery, have steadily increased pitchers' chances of getting back into action. Today, their chances are 90 in 100, and "Tommy John" surgery has saved the careers of more than 75 major leaguers!

A ~~Spoonful~~ OF PREVENTION...

...might make the number of injuries go down. Big-league teams try to protect pitchers from common elbow and shoulder injuries. Teams use a "starting rotation"—a schedule of starting pitchers—that gives pitchers time off to rest their arms between each game they play. Players do special exercises, like shoulder circles, to keep their shoulder muscles and sockets well-oiled and less injury-prone. Some do shoulder-strengthening exercises with J-Bands (see below), which fasten around their wrists and attach to a locker or railing, to help shrug off injuries before they start.

TIP

What's the best way to prevent baseball injuries? Warm up and stretch your muscles before you play. And don't forget to wear your protective gear—especially your batting helmet. A ball to the head can seriously scramble your brains.

Quick Hit

In the old days, many pitchers rubbed sore arms with "atomic balm"— ointment made from red-hot chili peppers. One time a little-leaguer got the shirt of Hall-of-Fame pitcher Sandy Koufax, who was a star of the early 1960s. When the kid put the shirt on, it was so hot from the burning balm that he thought he was on fire!

Pumped
UP ON DRUGS?

Are today's pros bigger, stronger, and smashing hitting records because they're taking steroids—drugs that help build larger muscles? That question hung over pro baseball like a black cloud in 2002, when former major leaguer Ken Caminiti admitted he took the drugs while he won the 1996 National League's Most Valuable Player award. Ken said half the players were on the stuff! Back then, major-league baseball had no rules about using steroids. Many fans thought something should be done. Not only do steroids have dangerous side effects, but they also give athletes an unfair advantage over competitors. It seems the big leagues agreed. In 2003, players agreed to be randomly tested for drugs. Now players who test positive for steroids and other perform-ance-boosting drugs get suspended for a number of games. If they test positive three times, they're banned from playing for life.

THE MIND

Flash forward 15 years: you are playing in the final game of the World Series. The team that wins will become baseball's champions of the world. The game is tied at the top of the ninth inning. Bases are loaded with two outs. Whether you see yourself on the mound delivering a wicked curveball to strike the batter out, or in the batter's box blasting the ball way out of the park, one thing's for sure: you need to be in great mental shape so your body can give it your best shot.

BASEBALL IS A HEAD GAME

Experts say that what separates great ball players from the rest is not physical ability, but the mind. Think about it: when you're in the batter's box or on the mound, you have time to think. For those few seconds, what you think can make or break your performance.

So put yourself in the scene described above. Are you telling yourself, "Don't blow it," and tensing up? Tense muscles hold you back from pitching or swinging to the best of your ability. Your confidence nosedives. Before you know it, you've psyched yourself out!

That's why top players play winning mind games. Instead of focusing on the score, or worrying about what they *don't* want to do, they focus on the little actions they want to achieve moment by moment. For example, as superstar hitter Pete Rose waited for each pitch, he said to himself, "See the ball, hit the ball," and his body remained relaxed and ready to swing with full power. Likewise, ace pitcher Tom Seaver helped change the New York Mets from lovable losers to a winning team by concentrating on throwing just "one pitch at a time."

By using your mind to focus on little actions in the here and now, you train it to help you achieve the goals you set. Then, one day your sharp mental tool may help you keep your cool, so you can play at the very top of your game and help your team win the World Series.

Quick Hit

According to Ty Cobb, one of the greatest hitters and base stealers of all time, "what's above the [player's] shoulders is more important than what's below."

DOWN IN THE SLUMP DUMPS?

So you're a starting pitcher and you've lost control of your fast-ball—it's zinging everywhere but where you want to put it. Or you're a hitter with a batting average over .300, but in the last 10 games you just haven't been able to connect with the ball. Sooner or later every player falls into a slump. The funny thing is, you may be throwing or swinging exactly the way you did before. Experts think slumps are not failures of skill, but mental traps that players fall into. To climb out of slumps, many pros focus on the basics. They take extra practice, or watch videos of their swing or delivery. If something's off, they fix it; if not, they can be confident their mechanics are bang-on. Other players take time off to completely clear their minds.

STAR ☆

When hitting sensation Ichiro Suzuki picked up a major-league bat in 2001, it was like a magic wand. Ichiro got 242 hits—more than any player in 71 years. But Ichiro's playing wizardry didn't come from magic. It came from a finely tuned mind. "The key is to always make sure you're in a normal mental state so you can play your normal game," he said. How does Ichiro park his mind in "normal"? Between the action, he glances at certain spots in the ballpark. Looking at those spots helps him make sure that his mind is working normally so he can turn in his best performance. It mentally prepares him to take the next step, er, base.

Ichiro Suzuki

GOTTA HAVE HEART

What's the one thing pro baseball players can't do without? Heart! Experts say you have to love the game to get to the major leagues. If you really want to play, you'll put in the hours to get in shape and master the skills of the game. You'll have fun doing it, too.

Play with heart, and you'll develop confidence in your skills. That confidence can make you mentally tough, so you can use those skills under pressure and be the best player you can be.

Take plucky shortstop David Eckstein (see below). A scout once told his father David would never make it to the major leagues. Some teams thought he was too small. And they thought his odd throw—David grips the ball with two fingers instead of three—was a liability. But David practiced as much as he could, believed in himself, and played all out. The Anaheim Angels took notice and put him in their regular lineup. Today, David's all-out play rubs off on his team-mates and lifts up the whole team.

The Wizard of Oz

Fans, players, and managers alike called him the Wizard. When shortstop Ozzie Smith took to the field from 1978 to 1996, he whirled into position doing handsprings and backflips. And his acrobatic flair didn't stop there. "Ooh! Aah!" went the crowd as Ozzie leaped to pluck the ball from midair, threw on the run, dove to glove grounders, then hopped to his knees to throw runners out. And the defensive Wiz turned somersaults to become a good hitter.

The Wizard's "magical" defensive plays won him 13 Gold Glove fielding awards in a row—a feat that most top major leaguers can only dream about, let alone a player who didn't have a glove to play with as a kid. Money was tight when Ozzie was growing up—the first glove he ever had was a paper bag! But Ozzie has said that the paper bag helped him practice getting rid of the ball quickly. The kid Wiz also practiced by throwing a baseball over the roof then running around to catch it. Though he never did catch that over-the-roof ball, he said "it never stopped me from trying."

Ozzie's mind, heart, and courage to keep trying made him baseball's Wizard of Oz. When Ozzie was inducted into the Baseball Hall of Fame in 2002, he said his recipe for success was "the mind to dream that the Scarecrow cherished, a heart to believe that the Tin Man ached for, and the courage of the Lion to persevere."

Chapter 4

THE SCIENCE OF EXPLOSIVE MOVES

ZOOM! A fastball whizzes past the batter and—thump!—it slams into the catcher's mitt. "Strike!" hollers the umpire and the fans cheer the home-team pitcher.

A batter swings and—crack!—belts the ball up, up, and away over the fence! "Ohhh!" gasp the fans.

Throwing fastballs and smashing homers are the most explosive moves in baseball. The fastest of the major-league pitchers fire fastballs at 160 km/h (100 mph) or more. And sluggers blast home runs more than 130 m (400 ft) through the sky. What makes these moves so explosive? It's the force and energy that players put into them. Hang onto your seat for a close-up look at how a fastball gets its speed and how a bat swing gets its power.

Have a Blast! ➢

SPECIAL DELIVERY

The fastball is the basic weapon of almost every pitcher's firepower. It's the easiest pitch to throw and control, as well as being a building block for several other pitches. Check out the split-second moves of winding up and delivering a pitch.

Facing the Batter

The pitcher faces home plate with her pivot foot (right foot for righties and left foot for southpaws) on the pitching rubber. She keeps the ball in her glove so the batter can't see her grip, which might give away what pitch she's about to hurl.

Stepping Back

The pitcher winds up to throw with the force of her whole body—the greater the energy she can put into the ball, the faster it will go! She steps behind the pitching rubber with her striding foot (opposite of the pivot foot). It's not a big step or she may lose her balance.

Balancing to Explode

She turns her pivot foot sideways along the rubber and lifts her striding knee to her chest. This is the balance point: her head is directly over her pivot foot.

Quick Hit

Once batters are on base, pitchers skip the full wind-up because it can give runners time to steal bases.

Loading Up

The pitcher begins to shift her weight toward home plate. She plants her striding foot with toes pointing at home plate as she brings her arm up and back so her elbow is slightly higher than her shoulder and her wrist is cocked. The pitch is "loaded" when the ball is at its highest point and she's positioned to put the energy of her whole body into it.

Releasing the Ball

The pitcher focuses on the target—the catcher's mitt. Then she brings her throwing arm forward and fully extends it as she drives her hips and chest toward home plate to give her arm more power. This brings her pivot foot forward. And with her arm, wrist, and hand relaxed, she releases the ball.

Following Through

The pitcher sweeps her throwing arm across her body and swings her glove hand back. Her pivot foot continues forward until it is next to, or slightly in front of, her striding foot. Following through helps her throw with all her force, and brings her into an ideal fielding position—weight balanced over both feet, knees bent, and glove ready.

GETTING A GRIP

Some pitches can foil batters because they look like fastballs but don't behave like them. But no matter what pitch hurlers pull out of their glove, it all starts with the grip. Check out how different grips make the ball move.

Fastball

This grip over four seams makes the ball spin about 1600 times a minute and shoot toward home plate in a straight line. Batters who connect with it often hit popups and flyball outs.

Sinker

The sinker, or two-seam fastball, is slower than the four-seam fastball. The ball sinks in the strike zone, often turning hits into ground ball outs.

Split-Fingered Fastball

When hurlers grip the ball with their fingerpads as shown, it zips toward the batter at knee height then drops suddenly as it crosses the plate.

Changeup

Thrown with a circle grip, the change-up heads for home plate like a fastball, but 15 km/h (10 mph) slower. It can fool batters into swinging early, fouling, or hitting weak grounders.

Slider

The slider looks like a fastball until it reaches the hitter, where it slides sharply to the side.

Curveball

Not only does the curveball break (move to the side), but it also drops—all in the last 4 or 5 m (13–16 ft) before home plate.

Knuckleball

Actually gripped by the fingertips, the knuckleball can swerve, jump, curve, dance, or rise on its way to the plate. Even the pitcher may have no idea where it's going to go!

Hey ace, don't start throwing curveballs until you're 13, when experts say your arm is ready.

When a big-league slugger swats a home run, the speed of the bat—about 120 km/h (75 mph)—gives it power. The ball squashes to half its size on impact, then springs back to its round shape and rockets away. How do the pros swing with such zing? Check out the mechanics of a full swing and see.

Setting Up

The batter stands next to home plate with feet about shoulder-width apart and knees bent, balancing his weight over both feet. His head is turned so he can watch the pitcher with both eyes. His grip on the bat is firm but not too tight—tension in his muscles may slow down his wrists and hands, robbing his swing of power. He holds the bat about 13 to 18 cm (5–7 in) away from his body, with his hands cocked just below his shoulder.

Loading Energy

Once the pitcher drops his hand behind him to begin the throw, the batter locks his eyes on the ball. As the pitcher releases the ball, the batter shifts his weight to his back foot. His body weight is stored energy, and this loads it up to give the bat speed and power.

Stepping into the Pitch

The batter pushes off his back foot and takes a small step forward with his front foot, planting it firmly. This step releases stored energy. It allows him to turn his hips and torso forward as he begins bringing the bat around.

Rotating at the Plate

The batter's hips and torso really get into the swing of things, rotating toward the pitch. His arms and hands transfer this rotational energy to the bat as he pulls it around—the bat can go from 30 km/h (20 mph) to 110 km/h (70 mph)! All the while, the batter keeps his head still and his eyes on the ball. He's aiming to swat the ball in front of home plate, where it's more likely to stay fair.

Following Through

The batter continues arcing the bat around over his opposite shoulder even if he has hit the ball. Following through helps him keep his balance and swing with power—swinging *through* the ball, and not just to the ball. It also helps ensure that all his moves up to this point are perfectly in tune. After all, once the pitcher releases the ball, the batter's got less than half a second to make a full swing.

TIP

When you take your position in the batter's box, check that your bat will cover the whole plate when you swing—or some pitches may be completely out of reach. Swing your bat across the plate or touch its tip to the outside corner. And if it doesn't reach all the way, adjust your position until it does.

The EXPLOSIVE Science of Baserunning

O nce sluggers hit the ball, they become baserunners without a second to spare. To avoid getting tagged out, major leaguers explode out of the batter's box and hotfoot it to first base in about 4 seconds.

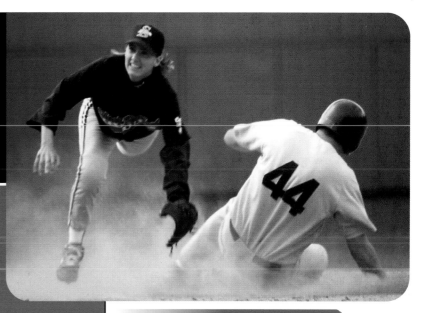

Running Through

Major leaguers don't run to first base, they run through it, so they don't slow down before they reach it.

Sliding

Since players can't overrun second or third base, the quickest way to stop on target is to slide feet-first from 2 to 3 m (7–10 ft) out. Dropping in low like this also helps pros dodge tags. Sometimes, sliding even has the added bonus of shaking the ball out of the fielder's glove.

Brainpower

Good major-league baserunners often use their heads more than their legs. They keep track of the number of outs, the opposition's positions in the field, and the ball. That way they can take big leads off bases without getting picked off, return to a base if a flyball is caught, and spot chances to run extra bases.

Stealing

Pro base thieves eye the opposition in the field to see who throws slowly and who throws fast. They also study the pitcher, as his moves might give away if he's going to pitch or to throw to first and pick off the runner. When they're on base, sly stealers use this information to figure out when they can explode down a basepath to steal without getting caught. Sneaky!

Quick Answers to **Hard-Hitting** Questions

Why do left-handed batters have an edge?

In the batter's box, lefties stand closer to first base than righties do. At the end of their swing, they are already moving toward the base. So a lefty can get there faster than a righty.

Why isn't a fastball always a pitcher's best bet?

Some fastballs speed toward home plate in a straight line. So, once hitters know where to look for them, they're off to the races, er, bases. That's why changing speeds and pitches to keep batters guessing is good pitching strategy.

LEGENDS OF THE GAME

The Splinter's Hitting Science

Teddy Ballgame, the Kid, the Thumper. Ted Williams was called them all. But no name stuck to the tall, skinny player with the picture-perfect swing quite like the Splendid Splinter. Ted set out to become the "greatest hitter who ever lived." And in the minds of many that's just what he did—especially in 1941.

With just one doubleheader left to go in the season, Boston Red Sox manager gave Ted the option of sitting out the two final games, so that his batting average (percentage of hits from all his times at bat) would round up to .400 for the season—an 11-year record. Sit out?! Ted wouldn't think of it. He'd been practicing for this moment all his life. Ever since he was a kid, he had been swinging bats— or rolled up newspapers, pillows, even shoes—every chance he got. Ted played and got six hits for eight at-bats, raising his season's batting average to .406—a feat no other player has matched since.

Hitting a baseball is "the hardest thing to do in sports," Ted often said. But he made it look easy—by turning it into a science. Ted's first rule of hitting was to get a good ball to hit. And he mapped out the strike zone to figure out his own "happy zone," where he could hit .400 or better. Now that's better batting through science!

Chapter 5

PITCHER vs. BATTER

On your mark, get set, duel!

Maybe that's what the ump should say instead of "Play ball!" Every game, pitchers and batters go to battle in a contest of skill, will, and wit.

But it's not an even match. Experts say the pitcher has the edge. The pitcher chooses exactly how to put the ball in play, and has eight players as back-up to field a ball if a batter gets good wood on it—something that happens only three times out of ten in the major leagues. So just what keeps a batter going? Hall-of-Famer Ty Cobb, who had 4,189 career hits, said "Every great batter works on the theory that the pitcher is more afraid of him than he is of the pitcher." Check out how pitchers and batters try to put the moves on each other.

Showdown Dead Ahead >

The duel of pitcher vs. batter isn't a one-shot deal like a penalty kick or shot in soccer or hockey. And most of the action happens in an imaginary box! Here's how diamond duels go down.

THE STRIKE ZONE

Zoom in on the strike zone—an imaginary box where duels are won or lost. But it's not always in the same spot. The Official Baseball Rules define the strike zone as the area above home plate measured from the batter's chest to the bottom of her knees. So it can vary from batter to batter and from pitch to pitch, depending on how much a batter crouches.

THE COUNT

The duel between the pitcher and the batter is based on the count: the number of balls the pitcher throws vs. the number of strikes the batter gets. Balls are pitches out of the strike zone that the batter doesn't swing at. Strikes are pitches in the strike zone that the batter doesn't swing at, pitches the batter swings at and misses, and fouls (hits that end up in foul territory). If the batter gets *three* strikes, he's out. But the pitcher can throw *four* balls before the batter gets a walk—a free trip to first base. Sound unfair? Well, if the batter has two strikes, he can hit any number of uncaught fouls before striking out, hitting, or walking.

WHO MAKES THE CALL?

Who decides whether a pitch is a ball or a strike? The ump, of course! An umpire stands behind the catcher at home plate to judge each pitch fairly. What he says, goes—even if his version of the strike zone is different from the Official Rules. Experts say many umps call the strike zone lower than the rules—from just above the batter's waist to the middle of the calf. And, while the zone's width is supposed to be the same as home plate, 43 cm (17 in), some umps seem to stretch it, while others shrink it. Those with wide plates are known as "pitcher's umpires" and those with skinny ones, "batter's umpires."

Using Your Head When You're Ahead

Once pro batters and pitchers figure out where the ump's strike zone is, they can stretch or shrink it like a rubber band to try to get an edge. Sound mental? It is, since the strike zone shifts only in their heads. Here's how.

Throwing a Shifty Trick

If the pitcher is ahead in the count—has fewer balls than the batter has strikes—she might stretch out the strike zone as much as 5 cm (2 in) on each side of the plate. Why? Once batters fall behind in the count, they're more likely to chase after pitches, trying to get a hit. So the pitcher pitches outside the strike zone to bait the batter to go after the pitch, which may be hard-to-reach, easy to miss, and tough to hit with much power.

Hitting a Shifty Trick

A batter who is ahead in the count—has fewer strikes than the pitcher has balls—can shrink the strike zone a bit off the outside edge, not swinging at pitches in that area or beyond. What's up with that? By laying off pitches there, the batter makes use of the fact that the pitcher doesn't want to get behind in the count. This can force the pitcher to throw the ball over the plate for strikes, giving the batter a pitch he can whack a long, long way with the sweet part of his bat.

And the Winner Is...

The batter...

- if the batter hits the ball and gets on base before being tagged out.
- if the batter gets a base on balls.
- if the batter gets a base on a hit-by-pitch.

The pitcher...

- if the pitcher strikes out the batter.
- if the batter hits the ball and gets tagged out, or a fielder catches the ball before it touches the ground.

Quick Hit

Until 1887, batters could request whatever type of pitch they felt like hitting! They would place an order for a high, fair, or low pitch with the umpire, who gave it to the pitcher.

CHOOSE YOUR (SECRET) WEAPON · · · · · · · ·

Hey, ace! Hey, slugger! If someone pointed at a spot on the plate or field and said, "Put it there," could you pitch or hit the ball that precisely? It's all a matter of control. Check out how pro pitchers and batters use control of the ball as a secret weapon to control the game—or at least some situations in the game!

PITCHER PERFECT CONTROL

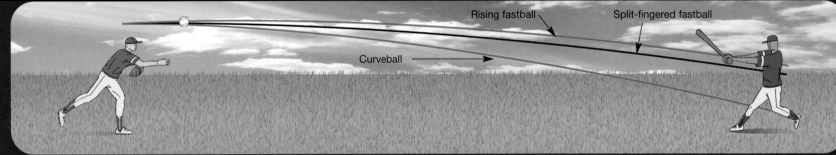

Rising fastball

Split-fingered fastball

Curveball

Want to know the secret to knock-'em-out—er, strike-'em-out—pitching? Control. If a pitcher can throw the ball where she wants to, when she wants to, she's got what it takes to put batters away. And there's a lot more to control than just throwing the ball through the strike zone. Top major-league pros can weave the ball through the inside and outside lanes, or edges, of the plate. They can place the ball high and low and everywhere in between. This kind of pinpoint control allows them to hurl the ball into hard-to-reach places, which can throw the batter off balance. And when this control is combined with the ability to change speeds (to upset a batter's timing), plus spin (to propel the ball on different paths), it can turn a pitcher into a true ace who rules the diamond.

TRY THIS!

Want to develop pitcher perfect control and turn your fastball into four different weapons?

YOU WILL NEED
- outdoor wall
- chalk
- rubber ball the size of a baseball
- glove

1 Imagine home plate on the ground in front of the wall. Draw the strike zone on the wall: the top at your chest and the bottom just below your knee. Make the box the same width as the plate—about 43 cm (17 in). Draw lines to divide the zone into four equal areas.

2 Now set up about 14 m (46 ft) from the wall—the Little League pitching distance from the mound to the plate.

3 Throw ten fastballs to the bottom left corner; ten to the bottom right; ten to the top left; and ten to the top right.

4 Keep practicing like this until you can hit each target every time. Then try these pitches in a game.

HITTING TO ALL FIELDS

***T**hwack! Whack! Smack!* Many hitting machines—like Wade Boggs and Tony Gwynn, who racked up more than 3000 big-league base hits each—can hit to all fields. This puts the element of surprise on the batter's side (since the opposition doesn't know where the hit will go), and allows a batter to go after different kinds of pitches.

Pulling the Ball

Smack!—the ball is "pulled" to left field by a right-handed pro (or right field by a left-handed hitter). Hitting a pitch coming at the inside edge before it reaches the plate can pull the ball. And some pull hitters, like Mark McGwire, pack lots of power!

Up the Middle

Whack! shoots a line drive—a hit that travels in a straight line—right up the middle of the park. If a pitch slices through the middle of the plate, batters often slam it up the center, aiming the ball "through the middle."

Opposite Field

Thwack! blasts the ball to the field facing the batter (right-field for righties and left-field for lefties). When a pitch comes in near the outside edge of the plate, pros can wait for the ball to get to them, then swat it to the opposite field.

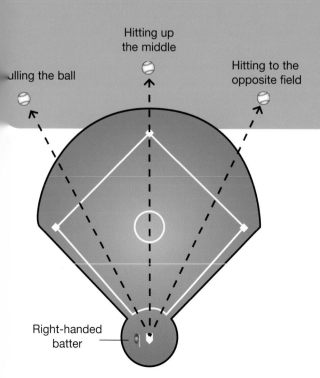

Hitting up the middle

Hitting to the opposite field

Pulling the ball

Right-handed batter

TRY THIS!

Want to become a spray hitter who can hit to all fields?

YOU WILL NEED

- batting helmet • bat
- baseball • pitcher with a glove

1 Have the pitcher throw you ten warm-up pitches.

2 Have the pitcher throw ten pitches down the middle of the plate. Try to hit the ball up the middle.

3 Have the pitcher throw ten near the outside edge. Try to hit the ball farther back on the plate, sending it to the opposite field.

4 Have the pitcher throw ten near the inside edge. Try to pull the ball by hitting it in front of the plate.

DUEL AT THE PLATE

The pitcher vs. batter duel is baseball's fuel. The game runs on it, players "do or die" on it, and fans eat it up. It's just you against the pitcher and her army of fielders. Or you against the hitter and his mighty swinging bat. Sound nerve-wracking? Relax. The key is to be prepared.

THE BATTER

Know your opponent

Does this pitcher have a zippy fastball, a sly changeup, or a drop-when-you-least-expect-it sinker? What pitch has he thrown that got you out? How will you handle it if he throws it this time? What "stuff" is he throwing well today?

See the ball

Lock your eyes on the ball as soon as the pitcher releases it, then track it as it rockets toward you. Your eyes try to recognize the pitch and send the information to your brain, which gears your body to swing or not. The secret is to keep your head still while you swing. If your head bobs around, the info your eyes send to your brain will be scrambled and, chances are, your swing will be too.

Get ahead in the count

Whoever gets ahead in the count often wins the duel. So don't swing at the first pitch—or any other—unless it's over the plate. If you won't be baited by balls off the plate, the pitcher may be forced to throw you a pitch you can slam!

Take your best swing

If you're behind in the count, don't change your approach because you think you've "gotta get a hit." The duel's not over till it's over.

Plan your attack

Step into the batter's box with a plan. If you know your opponent and can get ahead in the count (see above), you can wait for a pitch you can blast with your bat. By the fifth or sixth inning, hitters have had a chance to see exactly what stuff's working for the pitcher and what's not. So they may have an even better plan to beat him!

THE PITCHER

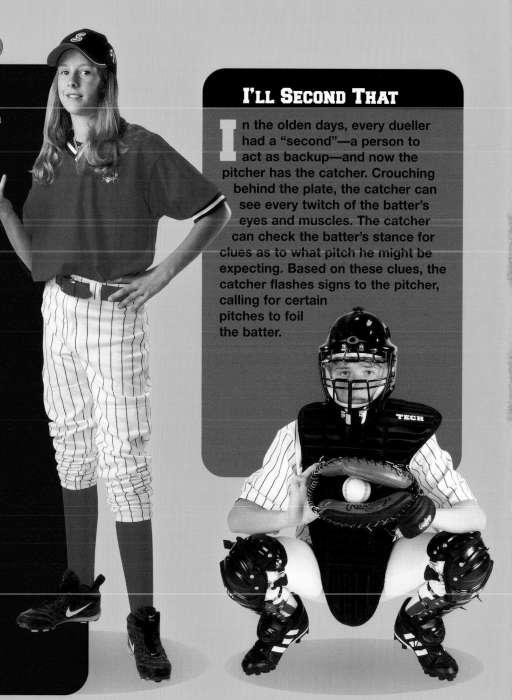

Know your opponent

Does this batter usually swing at the first pitch so you can throw a hard-to-reach ball for a strike? If you've faced her before, what did you throw that she hit a long way?

See the mitt

When pro pitchers are in the zone—throwing the ball exactly where they want to—they often say all they see is the catcher's mitt. By focusing on the target, you can throw through *to* the catcher rather than *at* the batter. This ensures that your pitch isn't short, and that surprise action you plan on happens at the plate, not before it, where the batter might do something about it.

Get ahead in the count

Whoever gets ahead in the count often wins the duel. So try to make your first pitch a strike. Put it where it's hard to hit—high and tight (near the batter), or low and away.

Throw your best stuff

You've heard the scouting report on what this batter's weak spots are. So it makes sense to pitch to them, no? No—not if those pitches aren't your best stuff. Go with your strengths, not the hitter's reported weaknesses. Throw your best pitch and dare her to make contact.

Throw outside—and inside

Develop control so you can mix up your pitches on the outside and inside lanes of home plate. If you always throw outside, batters will lean over the plate with the sweet part of their bat. But if you follow a few outside pitches with an inside pitch, they'll be a lot less likely to lean over for fear of getting hit by the ball.

I'LL SECOND THAT

In the olden days, every dueller had a "second"—a person to act as backup—and now the pitcher has the catcher. Crouching behind the plate, the catcher can see every twitch of the batter's eyes and muscles. The catcher can check the batter's stance for clues as to what pitch he might be expecting. Based on these clues, the catcher flashes signs to the pitcher, calling for certain pitches to foil the batter.

LEGENDS OF THE GAME

Few Could Outmatch Satch

No pitcher could throw down a challenge like Leroy "Satchel" Paige. The cool right-handed ace played in the Negro Leagues from the 1920s to the 1940s, when players of color weren't allowed in the major leagues. Legend has it that he once had all his outfielders sit down while he pitched to Josh Gibson (known as the "black Babe Ruth")—Satch's way of saying, "I don't need any backup, because you're not going to hit a thing."

In another game, Satch told Gibson he was going to strike him out with the bases loaded. In the ninth inning with one player on, Satch wound up, kicking his front leg to the sky in his unique style, and walked two batters to load the bases before Gibson stepped into the batter's box. Then Satch turned to the 30,000 fans in the stands and told them he was going to give Gibson three fastballs. Maybe Satch's confidence threw the slugger off balance—Satch blew three fastballs right by Gibson for three strikes to end the game.

Players, including major leaguers who faced Satch in exhibition games, said he was the greatest pitcher in baseball. They said that "he threw fire," and that he wound up with a baseball but threw a pea. In any case, Satch toyed with batters' heads, psyching 'em out to strike 'em out!

Chapter 6

PLAYING BY NUMBERS

CRUNCH!

Pro baseball's number crunchers are at it again. Each game, the Official Scorer enters the number of hits, pitches, strikeouts, walks, fielding errors, doubles, home runs—and, of course, the score—onto a scorecard. Stats keepers crunch the numbers to calculate up-to-the-minute win—loss percentages, batting averages, ERAs, and RBIs.

Percentages, averages, ER-whats, and RB-whys? The game's numbers and statistics—stats for short—are serious stuff, all written in code. They help managers measure up individual players' performances, compare players, determine salaries, and set strategy during games. Check out how to crack the code and play by the numbers.

Zero In...

Barry Bonds is the "bomb." In 2001, he banged out 73 home runs in a single season, wiping out Mark McGwire's record of 70. See Bonds' stats (below) from that remarkable season, and what batters' numbers say about their performance. Bonds didn't stop hitting there. In 2007, he shattered Hank Aaron's long-standing record of 755 career home runs. But some people say that Bonds' play has been helped by performance-enhancing drugs, so his records are tarnished. Bonds says he has never knowingly used steroids. What do you think? Do Bonds' records stack up with the best? Is he the legitimate king of swing?

BA	SLG	OBA	G	AB	R	H	TB	2B	3B	HR	RBI	BB	SO
.328	.863	.515	153	476	129	156	411	32	2	73	137	177	93

BA Batting Average

This is *the* big number for hitters, measuring the percentage of at-bats that result in base hits. Hitting .300 (say "three-hundred") and above is considered good, and .400 is excellent. But experts say batting average isn't the last word on hitting ability, because it doesn't reveal whether the player can hit for power or pick up walks. Do the math by dividing the hits by at-bats: $BA = H \div AB = 156 \div 476 = .328$

SLG Slugging Average

This stat reveals a hitter's power—the average number of bases the hitter reaches each at-bat. The typical major leaguer has a slugging average around .420, and top sluggers .490 or more. With a slugging average of .863, Bonds set a major-league record. Figure it out by dividing the total bases by number of at-bats: $SLG = TB \div AB = 411 \div 476 = .863$

OBA On-Base Average

The on-base average is the batting average with walks and hit-by-pitches counted in. It tells you the percentage of plate appearances the batter gets on base, period. So some pro managers think it's a better measure of a batter's offensive skill than batting average, since you can't score runs without getting on base. Experts say a high OBA often reveals an aggressive batter—Barry's .515 is the highest since Ted Williams' .526 in 1957.

G Games played

AB At-Bats

A player going to bat doesn't always count as an at-bat. (Stats can drive you batty!) When a hitter gets a hit, strikes out, or gets on base due to an error or fielder's choice (to throw out a runner rather than the hitter), it counts as an at-bat. But if the hitter gets a walk, gets hit by a pitch, or hits a sacrifice bunt or fly, it doesn't. Since at-bats are used to calculate batting average, only the batter's trips to the plate resulting in hits affect the batting average.

R Runs scored

H Hits

TB Total Bases

This is the number of bases a batter racks up in all his at-bats. A single hit counts for one base, a double for two bases, a triple for three, and a homer for four.

2B Doubles

These are hits that get the batter to second base.

3B Triples

Hits that get the batter to third base.

HR Home Runs

Barry's 73 long balls broke the record for the most home runs in a season.

RBI Runs Batted In

"Ribbies" or "ribeyes" are a big part of every batter's job. A batter gets an RBI when she drives a runner home with a hit, a bunt or fly that puts herself out, a walk, a fielder's choice, or an error. She also chalks one up if she hits herself home with a home run.

BB Bases-on-Balls or walks

Is 177 a staggering number of walks? You bet! In 2001, Barry strolled past legendary slugger Babe Ruth's 1923 record of 170. And the next year, he shuffled beyond the record again, collecting 198 walks. A record 68 of those were intentional walks—more than the total walks of any of Barry's teammates!

SO Strikeouts

Strikeouts are a fact of every batter's life, including a superstar's. The average big leaguer gets whiffed at the plate about twice in every 11 times at bat.

SB Stolen Bases

CS Caught Stealing

E Errors

SB	CS	E
13	3	6

BATTING IN ORDER

Skill, strategy, science, and "stat sense": here's how they add up to create a team's batting order.

The Kick, er Hit, Starters

1 The lead-off batter must get on base as often as possible. Batters with high BAs and OBAs are put in this spot.

2 Traditionally, this batter's mission is to get on base and move batter #1 ahead through well-placed hits. But mathematicians have found that placing the team's top slugger here can improve the results of up to 10 games per season! Batting earlier in the order gives the best batter more chances to bat.

The Heart of the Order

3 In this spot, managers look for a batter who is high on RBIs and homers to drive #1 and #2 home for runs.

4 The top slugger traditionally fills this "cleanup" spot, and hits runners home.

5 The fifth batter's job is to drive any left-over runners home.

The "In-Betweeners"

6 & 7 After the heart of the order shakes things up, managers look for steady hitters who can get on base.

The Bottom of the Order

8 Players stronger on defense than offense—with low batting averages but high fielding percentages—are here.

9 In the National League, the pitcher is the last batter. In the American League, a designated hitter, or DH, bats instead of the pitcher, anywhere in the lineup.

Quick Hit

Hank Aaron's home-run record was untouched for 31 years. But as soon as Bonds smashed it in 2007, people were already talking about who would break the new record.

Barry Zito's not your average pitcher. For one thing, he's a lefty, and lefties' curveballs curve the opposite way from righties'. For another, he's deadly accurate. In 2002 Zito led the American League in wins and bagged the Cy Young award for outstanding pitching. Check out Barry's award-winning season's stats and see how a pitcher's numbers add up.

W	L	ERA	G	GS	SV	IP	H	R	ER	HR	HBP	BB	SO
23	5	2.75	35	35	0	229.1	182	79	70	24	9	78	182

W Wins

Winning games is what pitching is all about, so this is the big number for pitchers. Starting pitchers like Barry get credit for a win if they throw for at least five innings *and* their team has the lead when they're relieved *and* the team wins without losing the lead. Top pitchers have a steady winning percentage of .600 or more. You can work out winning percentage like this:
$W \div (W + L) = 23 \div (23 + 5) = .821$

L Losses

No pitcher likes to count his losses—unless he can count them on one hand. When major-league teams lose, the loss goes to the pitcher who gives up the go-ahead run that defeats the team.

ERA Earned Run Average

A pitcher's ERA tells you how many earned runs—runs the opposing team gets through hits, walks, and hit-by pitches (but not fielding errors)—the pitcher gives up every nine innings. So the lower it is, the better. Here's how to do the math:
$(ER \times 9 \text{ innings}) \div IP = (70 \times 9) \div 229.1 = 2.75$

G Games played

GS Games Started

SV Saves

Zero saves for Zito? If you figure it's because Barry is a starter, you're right on the ball! Only relief pitchers get saves, or wins they pull out of the jaws of defeat.

IP Innings Pitched

H Hits allowed

R Runs scored against

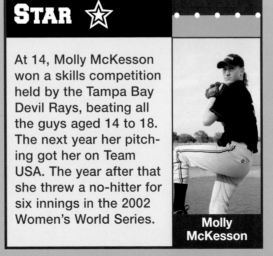
ER Earned Runs

This counts any runs that come about from the pitcher's play (unearned runs come about from errors or moves made by fielders or the catcher).

HR Home Runs given up

HBP Hit-By-Pitches

The number of pitches that hit batters. Ow! The batter's revenge is that he automatically goes to first base.

BB Bases on Balls or walks

SO Strikeouts

Barry whiffed a good number of batters in 2002. Legendary flamethrower Nolan Ryan, known as the Ryan Express because his fastball traveled so fast, struck out a record-setting 383 in 1973.

What's the 40-40 club?

A small group of players who hit 40 or more home runs and stole 40 or more bases in the same season. Jose Canseco started the club in 1988. By 2007 Alex Rodriguez, Barry Bonds, and Alfonso Soriano were its only other members.

Does the home-run record still count?

In 1961, Roger Maris belted a remarkable 61 long balls. This record stood until 1998, when Mark McGwire and Sammy Sosa ripped through the record—Sammy with 66 homers for the season and Mark with 70. Then in 2001, Barry Bonds walloped a whopping 73 round-trippers, becoming the new home-run king. And while the action had some fans on the edge of their seats, it put others to sleep. They said the home-run record didn't mean much any more because hitting home runs had become too easy. What do you think?

When is a play an error?

When the Official Scorer says so! Every major-league game is watched carefully by an Official Scorer hired by the league to decide whether errors have been made on plays.

Jolting Joe Does the Impossible

"**D**id he get a hit? Did he?! *Did he?!*" That was the question on the minds of baseball fans during the summer of 1941. On May 15, Joe DiMaggio, right-handed centerfielder for the New York Yankees, went on a hot hitting streak, clobbering the ball for at least one safe hit every game. Soon baseball stats keepers were digging up streak records for him to break.

And Jolting Joe and his bat kept knocking those records down. The red-hot hitter shattered the Yankee record of hits in 29 consecutive games, and pounded Wee Willie Keeler's 44-game hitting streak from 1897 into the dust. When DiMaggio's streak finally ended on July 17, as spectacular fielding plays robbed Joe of a base hit not once but three times, Joe had at least one hit in 56 straight games.

Experts think Jolting Joe's 56-game hitting streak may be the most remarkable feat in all of pro sports. For starters, it stands head and shoulders above the previous record, and no batter has even come close ever since. What's more, scientists who have calculated the chance, or likelihood, of the streak happening, say it "shouldn't have happened at all." Joe DiMaggio's impossible hitting streak defies the odds of chance. Well, it could only happen in baseball!

Chapter 7

TAKE ME OUT TO THE BALLPARK

Nothing beats

going to the ballpark and watching your favorite team take on the opposition. Where else can you cheer like thunder, spy sweat fly, and sit in a field of dreams?

There's no place like it—not even another ballpark. Every major-league ballpark is different, and that affects how the game plays out. For example, not all ballpark fences are the same distance from home plate, so hits that are deep fly balls in one can be home runs in another.

When pros play on the road, they do a pre-game check of the opponents' "turf" to see how the ball comes off the ground, corners, and fences. Of course, every home team knows their own ballpark inside out. Read on to get the home-field advantage.

Get Your
Ticket Here...

Think fast: what do ballparks have in common with players? Personality! Each ballpark has a unique character, and their quirks can really rule the game.

WHERE THE GREEN MONSTER RULES

Beware of the Green Monster that looms over left field at Fenway Park, home of the Boston Red Sox. The 11-m (37-ft) tall wall has a nasty reputation for bedeviling fielders and hitters alike. Standing only 94 m (310 ft) from home plate, the Green Monster can stop hits in midflight and fling them back so wildly that no one has any idea where they'll end up. In the old days, the Monster snared weak fly balls in an upper fence, turning them into home runs, and its frame of wooden planks was covered in tin. If the ball struck a plank it would bounce back toward the infield, but if it struck tin it would drop straight down to the ground. Today, the Green Monster is made of hard plastic inside and out. But maybe the giant wall makes the Red Sox feel at home. Talk of designing a new ballpark includes a plan to stick him in the very same spot.

BALLS VANISH INTO THIN AIR

Up, up, and away! That's where many hits go at Coors Field in Denver. When the field opened in 1995, hitters scored twice as many runs there as at any other ballpark. It's hitter's heaven— 2.5 km, or "a mile high," in the sky— because the air is thinner up there. As the ball travels through the air, the air pushes against it, slowing it down. Thinner air pushes against the ball less, so hits travel about 10% farther.

The thin air at Coors Field is also drier, and so it dries out the ball. The home-team Colorado Rockies started storing the balls in a temperature- and moisture-controlled room in 2002. The result? The average number of runs per game dropped from an out-of-this-world 15 to a more earthbound 10. Moister balls are heavier and less bouncy, so they don't travel as far when they're hit.

A Goofy Roof

Tracking fly balls against the roof of the Minnesota Twins Metrodome is no easy job. Oakland A's first baseman Scott Hatteberg once said the white fabric roof is "exactly the color of a dirty baseball." So visiting outfielders often lose sight of the ball and goof up plays. One time, the ball didn't come back down at all. In 1984, Dave "King Kong" Kingman ripped the ball through a hole in the roof. The hit was out of the park, but the ump ruled it was only a double, not a homer.

STAR ☆

Yankee Stadium was especially designed for superstar Babe Ruth. The lefty power hitter blasted home runs into the right center bleachers, which became known as Ruthville. Eventually, the stadium was nicknamed the House that Ruth Built.

Yankee Stadium

FENCES THAT WALK

Major-league fences look upstanding, but they've been known to get shifty—or shifted. In 1949, Frank Lane, general manager of the White Sox, had the right- and left-field fences of his team's park moved in about 6 m (22 ft). But when the weak-hitting Senators came to town for three games, the two teams hit a whopping 14 homers, so Frank had the fences moved back. That's when the big leagues ruled that a team may not move its fences or alter the playing field in any other way during the season.

Blowing in the Wind

During a 1961 All-Star Game, the wind that blew into the home ballpark of the San Francisco Giants scooped relief pitcher Stu Miller right up off the mound! The stands in most ballparks shield fields from such strong gusts, but lighter winds still blow. Pro pitchers check which way the wind is blowing: if it's blowing at their back it can add zip to their fastball; but if it's blowing in their face it might whittle away some of their fastball's speed. Pro hitters also get a feel for the wind. If it's at their back in the batter's box, they may decide to swing for the fences, hoping the ball will ride on the wind. But if it's blowing against them, they may try to hit a line drive to slice through it. And if the wind is blowing right or left, hitters may try to hit the same way so the ball travels farther. Now that's going with the flow, er, blow!

Quick Hit

Almost every ballpark has seats without any backrests located outside the outfield fences. They're called "bleachers" since fans can sit in them and bleach in the sun.

FIELD OF GREEN • • • • • • • •

In 1965, Judge Roy Hofheinz built the world's first indoor ballpark, the Houston Astrodome, and called it the "eighth wonder of the world." Wonder why—the grass in it died! So out rolled the AstroTurf, and it went on to carpet many parks. Today, grass is growing back in style, and many state-of-the-art ballparks, including those with roofs that open and close, have fields of grass. Makes you wonder if maybe there's nothing like the real thing!

FUNKY
on the Eyes

No, your eyes are not playing tricks on you. There really are stripes, stars, diamonds, and checkerboard patterns in the grass of big-league parks. They're not made with paint, different types of grass, or even by cutting the grass different heights. Groundskeepers create those funky designs with a reel mower, one that has a roller on the back. The roller bends the grass in the same direction as the mower moves. When you look at the field, the grass bending away from you looks light green and the grass bending toward you looks dark green. That's because sunlight reflects off the entire blades of the grass bending away from you, but only off the tips of the blades bending toward you. Mind-bending, isn't it?

No matter how you look at it, synthetic turf and real grass are just not the same to play on. Here's how the two stack up blade for blade:

- Synthetic turf speeds up the game. It lies on top of concrete rather than soil, so hits bounce faster and higher—toward or away from fielding players!

- The number of stolen bases shot up with AstroTurf. A faster game required faster fielders, who were fast around the bases, too.

- Synthetic turf is made of panels held together at the seams by zippers. If the ball hits one of the seams, it can hop unpredictably.

- If your skin rubs against synthetic turf, you can get patches of irritated skin, or carpet-burn. And turf, with only a layer of underpadding over concrete, has a lot less give than grass growing on dirt.

- Grass can cushion soft bunts to a stop. But those same bunts will likely roll on the "rug"—sometimes right to an opposing fielder.

PLAYING IN THE DIRT

Seventy percent of baseball's action takes place on the infield. And experts say the difference between a good infield and a lousy one lies in the dirt. Good dirt is usually a mix of sand, clay, and silt. Not just any mix will do: too much sand and the soil may sink down in heavy-traffic areas; too little sand and the field won't drain. Groundskeepers often start with a mix of 60% sand, 15% silt, and 20% clay, and then adjust from there to find what works best on their "turf." They even use different soil conditioners in different areas to make the field hard or soft, so each infielder gets to play on his field of dreams.

THE GRASS IS GREENER

You won't find major-league grass growing in your backyard. The designer grass that grows in major-league baseball's state-of-the-art ballparks is developed to suit the climate conditions of the individual park. It needs more nutrients and water, because the sand it's grown in doesn't hold them like soil. What the sand in a big-league ballpark does hold is almost 1 km (about ½ mile) of irrigation pipes. Below the sand are more than 8 km (5 miles) of drain pipes to take away excess water. They can also pump warm air through the ground in the spring to nudge the grass back to life earlier than Mother Nature!

Quick Hit

In the mid 1990s, groundskeepers at Tiger Stadium in Detroit gave their field an emergency dye job. Vegetable dye turned their brown grass emerald green!

BALLPARK SIGHTS

Keep your eye on the ball.
It sounds easy, right? Wrong!
But it's really important.

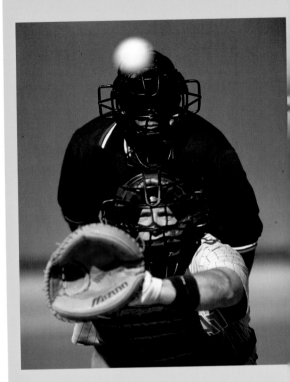

UMPS GET A HIGH-TECH EYE

Nobody has to keep their eye on the ball more than home-plate umpires. In 2001, major-league baseball began outfitting ballparks with high-tech help for the men in blue. The Umpire Information System (UIS) uses cameras to track the ball from the pitcher's hand to the plate, and to shoot the batter just after the pitch is thrown. The system combines all this visual information to model the flight of the ball and show whether it's a ball or a strike. After the game, it spits out a CD-ROM. By seeing how their game calls compare to UIS's, umps can sharpen their strike-zone judgement and keep their calls on the ball!

IN THE BLINK OF AN EYE

"Hit the dirt!" One night, that's what players at Griffith Stadium in Washington did. The lights went out during the pitcher's windup, and the pitcher was the only one who knew if he had thrown the pitch. So everyone else, including umpires and coaches, ducked to avoid getting nailed by the ball.

Sightlines are important for play as well as for safety. The Official Rules say it is desirable for ballparks to be laid out so the line from home plate through the pitcher's mound and second base runs east-northeast. That way batters don't have to face pitchers with the afternoon sun beaming into their eyeballs.

Fastballs on the Rise?

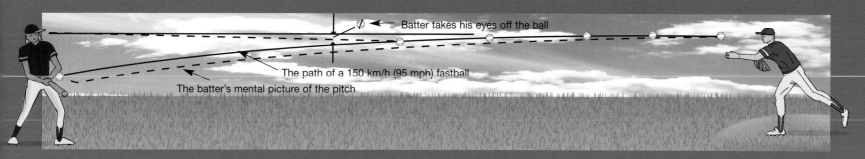

Batter takes his eyes off the ball

The path of a 150 km/h (95 mph) fastball

The batter's mental picture of the pitch

Many pro batters say fastballs sometimes rise just in front of home plate, hopping up while their bats cut through the air beneath them. According to scientists, the rising fastball is an optical illusion. They say it's not humanly possible for pitchers to throw the ball with enough backspin to make it rise against gravity—the natural force that attracts things to the earth—as it reaches the batter. Here's how the illusion might work. To hit a ball, the batter predicts where it will be at the plate. But if she underestimates its speed, she may expect the pitch to be lower than it is. The faster the fastball, the less time gravity has to pull it toward the ground, so the higher it will be. And if the batter takes her eyes off the ball to, say, focus on its impact point with her bat, the ball is higher than her mental picture of it when it crosses the plate. So the ball appears to hop up—and likely gets a rise out of the batter.

Quick Answers to Hard-Hitting Questions

Why put a left-handed pitcher against a left-handed batter?

When a lefty pitcher fires a curveball to a lefty player—or a right-handed pitcher to a right-handed batter—the ball veers away from the batter and is harder to hit. Also, a pitch that moves away from the batter might upset his balance. So, in close games, managers will bring in a pitcher who can use this advantage.

Does a curveball really curve?

Most players would say, "You bet!" And in 1870 pitcher Fred Goldsmith demonstrated a curveball that slalomed around three poles set in a straight line. Still, many scientists thought the swoop of a curveball was an optical illusion. In 1941, *Life* magazine took high-speed photos of pro pitchers' curveballs, but the editors didn't recognize the visual proof and reported that the pitch didn't curve at all! It took several scientific studies and a new set of photos in 1953 to convince them and, in turn, the rest of the world otherwise.

BALLPARK SOUNDS

Picture this: you are playing in the outfield and the ball is hit directly toward you—the toughest type of hit to judge. You look up to track its path, but for about two seconds, it's impossible to see whether the ball will bloop up over the infield or soar over your head. If you wait that long before running to catch it, you might not get there before it hits the grass. What do you do?

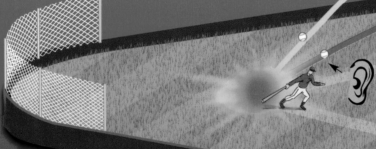

Short ball, 5 seconds to land

 Outfielder sees where the ball is going about 2 seconds after it's hit

Outfielder hears a solid or weak hit 0.3 seconds after the ball is hit

TUNING IN TO HITS

Believe it or not, pro outfielders' ears can tell them where the ball is going faster than their eyes can. The sound of the hit reaches them in 0.3 seconds. That's faster than the critical visual signs, so it can mean the difference between catching and missing the ball. "As soon as I hear the sound of the bat, I know where the ball is going," Melvin Mora, an outfielder for the Baltimore Orioles, told the *New York Times* in 2001. If he hears a *crack*, he runs back; if he hears a *clunk*, he charges in.

Physicist Dr. Robert Adair, a keen baseball fan who has studied the raucous sounds of ball and bat collisions, has found that the sharp **CRACK** and the dull **CLUNK** are two completely different sounds.

CRACK = Well-Hit Ball

The crack is heard when the bat's sweet spot, which propels the ball farther than any other part of the bat, hits the ball. The bat briefly flattens the ball and wraps itself around the ball, forcing out the air between them. As the air rushes out, it makes the sound of the crack.

Long ball, 4.3 seconds to land

Outfielder starts running when he sees where the hit's going

Misses ball

Misses ball

Catches ball

Catches ball

Outfielder starts running when he hears the hit

CLUNK = Weak Fly Ball

The clunk is heard when the ball is hit by the bat on either side of the sweet spot. When these parts of the bat connect with the ball, the bat vibrates like a plucked guitar string. These vibrations are too small for the human eye to see, but hitters can feel them as the bat stings their hands. The vibrations combine with the crack of the air rushing out to make a dull clunking sound.

CALL IT TEAMWORK

Ever notice that, when outfielders catch a ball at the fence, they usually throw it to an infielder instead of to home plate? They know that it will get there faster and with more accuracy through a cutoff guy or gal who relays it to the catcher. What's more, if a runner has already scored when the cutoff player gets the ball, a relay play can catch another runner out at second or third base, rather than giving runners time to reach base safely while the ball whiffles through the air all the way home. Now that's sound play!

STAR ☆

In the early 1900s, ear-splitting cheers greeted Lizzie Murphy, the Queen of Baseball. The owner of the men's semi-pro team she played first base for, the Boston All-Stars, had Lizzie's full name stitched on the front and back of her shirt, so fans could spot her on the field.

Lizzie Murphy

SOUND MATTERS!

⚾ Whoosh! Walter "the Big Train" Johnson, who played for the Washington Senators in the early 1900s, had a fastball so fast that hitters said they couldn't see it. They said they could only hear as it rumbled across the plate like a locomotive train. Apparently, it was very effective—the Big Train shut out hitters in a record 110 games.

⚾ Welcome to Thunderdome! Cheers and whoops of the Minnesota Twins' fans boomed throughout the Metrodome during the 1987 World Series, setting a sound record. When Twin hitter Dan Gladden hit a grand slam during the first game, a sound meter shot up to 118 decibels. That's as loud as a jet taking off! Is it any wonder the Twins took the World Series, winning four games at the Metrodome?

Winning Monkey Business

"If you make noise, he will come." In the 2002 World Series, that's what you would see flashing across the Anaheim Angels' scoreboard.

It all started on June 6, 2000. The Angels were losing to the San Francisco Giants in the sixth inning. The guys in Anaheim's scoreboard control room threw a movie clip of a monkey and the caption "Rally Monkey" up on the JumboTron. The fans went bananas, so the monkey went up each time the Angels were at bat. By the ninth inning, the team had rallied to trail the Giants by just one run. To calls of "Show the Monkey!" the Angels clinched the game. The next day, the Rally Monkey stirred up the crowd again, and the Angels came back to win again.

Soon fans were bringing stuffed monkeys to the ball-park. Anaheim hired a white-faced capuchin monkey actor, dressed him in an Angel's uniform, and filmed their own Rally Monkey clips. The Rally Monkey appears only after the sixth inning, and only if the Angels are losing—when they need him most. He popped up throughout the 2002 playoffs, as the Angels rallied from behind to win several games, and ultimately the World Series. Maybe it was a case of "monkey see, monkey do"!

THE FIELD AND PLAYERS

- The field has three areas: infield, outfield, and foul territory.

- Nine or ten players per team
- When a team is at-bat, it is on offense.

- When a team is in the field, it is on defense.

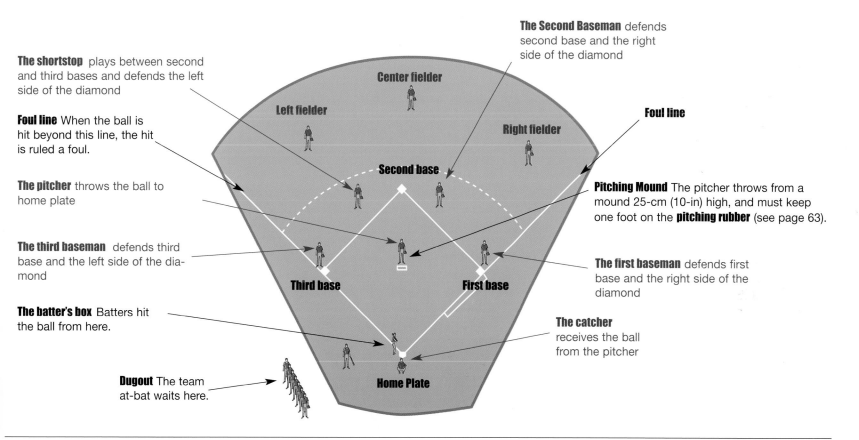

The shortstop plays between second and third bases and defends the left side of the diamond

Foul line When the ball is hit beyond this line, the hit is ruled a foul.

The pitcher throws the ball to home plate

The third baseman defends third base and the left side of the diamond

The batter's box Batters hit the ball from here.

Dugout The team at-bat waits here.

The Second Baseman defends second base and the right side of the diamond

Center fielder

Left fielder

Right fielder

Second base

Foul line

Pitching Mound The pitcher throws from a mound 25-cm (10-in) high, and must keep one foot on the **pitching rubber** (see page 63).

Third base

First base

The first baseman defends first base and the right side of the diamond

The catcher receives the ball from the pitcher

Home Plate

HOW TO PLAY

- The object of the game is to score runs by hitting the ball and advancing around the bases. The team with the most runs wins.

- There are nine innings in which each team has a turn at bat and a turn in the field. The visiting team bats first, at the top of the inning, and the home team bats at the bottom of the inning.

- A team is at-bat until three players get out by getting three strikes, not reaching a base before the ball, getting tagged with the ball, or hitting a ball that is caught before it touches the ground.

- The game cannot end in a tie. If the score is tied at the end of the ninth inning, full extra innings are played until the visiting team has more runs or the home team scores a winning run.

Ace – the top pitcher on a team

Advance – when a runner moves along the base paths; when a hitter moves a runner at least one base

At-bat – when a batter gets a hit, makes an out, or gets on base on an error or fielder's choice; walks, hit-by-pitches, sacrifice bunts and flies do not count as at-bats

Ball – a pitch that doesn't enter the strike zone and is not swung at by the batter

Base – one of three white canvas bags runners must touch as they try to reach home plate to score runs

Base on balls – when the batter gets a free trip to first base because the pitcher throws four balls

Baserunner – an offensive player running from base to base to try to score

Bases loaded – when a team has a runner on each of first, second, and third bases

Bat – a wooden or aluminum tool that players use to hit the ball; aluminum bats are not allowed in the major leagues

Batter – the offensive player in the batter's box

Batting average – the percentage of a hitter's at-bats that result in base hits

Batting order – the order in which a team's hitters go to the batter's box during a game

Bunt – a batted ball intentionally hit softly to remain in the infield

Catcher – fielder who plays behind home plate to receive the ball from the pitcher

Changeup – a pitch that looks like a fastball but is slower

Count – the number of balls and strikes thrown during an at-bat; the balls are listed first

Corked bat – an illegal bat in which a hole has been drilled and filled with cork

Curveball – a pitch that breaks, or moves, toward or away from the batter as it crosses the plate

Cutoff player or Relay player – a fielder who receives the ball from the fielder who caught it, and throws it to the catcher or another fielder

Dead ball – a ball that is out of play

Defense – the team in the field trying to prevent the opposition from scoring

Diamond – the infield

Doubleheader – two games played back to back

Double play – a play in which the defensive team puts out two offense players in continuous action

Earned run – a run the opposing team gets through a hit, walk, or hit-by-pitch, but not through a fielding error

Earned run average – the number of earned runs given up every nine innings

Fastball – a high-speed pitch

Fielder – any defensive player

Fielder's choice – when a fielder decides not to throw to first base to put out the batter-runner, but instead throws to another base to put out a preceding runner

Fly ball – a batted ball that flies high through the air

Foul – a batted ball that settles in foul territory; that is, outside the first or third base lines

Foul tip – a batted ball that goes directly to the catcher's hands and is caught legally

Grand slam – a home run when bases are loaded

Ground ball – a batted ball that rolls or bounces close to the ground

Hit-by-pitch – when the batter is hit by a pitch and is automatically awarded first base

Home run – a hit that allows the batter to run around all the bases to score; also can be called a homer, long ball, or round-tripper

Infield – the area of the playing field inside the baselines

Inning – a part of the game in which each team takes a turn on offense and defense

JumboTron – a giant video screen in ballparks

Knuckleball – a pitch that moves unpredictably

Line drive – a ball hit in a straight line through the air

Live ball – a ball that is in play

Major leagues or big leagues – the National League and American League of professional baseball teams in the United States and Canada

Mitt – the leather protective hand-covering worn by catchers and first basemen to help catch and handle the ball

No-hitter – a game in which the pitcher holds the opposition hitless

Offense – the team at bat trying to score runs

Official Scorer – a league-appointed official who observes the game, records the score and action, and decides whether plays are hits or errors

On-base average or On-base percentage – the percentage of plate appearances the batter gets on base

Out – a batter or runner put out of play by the opposition; once a team on offense gets three outs in an inning, it shifts to defense

Outfield – the area of the playing field beyond the bases

Overhand – thrown with the hand above the shoulder

Pick off – a throw by pitcher or catcher to put out a runner who is off base

Pitch – a ball delivered to the batter

Pitching rubber – a rectangular slab of white rubber the pitcher stands on

Pitcher – the fielder who delivers the ball to the batter

Plate appearances – trips to the plate by a hitter

Pop fly – a high but weak fly ball that usually stays within the infield

Relief pitcher or Reliever – a pitcher who plays after the starter is removed from the game

Rising fastball – a fastball that appears to rise, hop, or jump at the plate

Rosin – a dry powder that pitchers use to dust their hands (not the ball) for grip

Run – a score made by a player who advances around the bases, touching each base, and reaches home plate; teams get one point for each run

Runs batted in – when a batter drives a runner or himself home

Sacrifice bunt – when a hitter intentionally bunts out to advance a runner

Sacrifice fly – a fly ball hit far enough for a runner on third to score while the team has less than two out

Scuffball – an illegal pitch thrown with a ball that has been roughened up or scuffed, which makes the ball break, or move, toward the scuff

Set position – a legal pitching position in which the pitcher doesn't windup

Sinker – a fastball that sinks in the strike zone

Slide – when a runner drops down and reaches a base along the ground

Slider – a pitch that suddenly slides to the side

Slugger – a hitter who hits many home runs

Slugging average – total number of bases a hitter reaches through hits divided by number of at-bats

Southpaw – a left-handed pitcher

Spitball – an illegal pitch thrown with spit or any other slippery substance on the ball

Starter – a pitcher who starts games

Starting rotation – the playing schedule of a team's starting pitchers

Stolen base – a base the runner takes without being advanced by a batter

Strike – when the batter swings and misses, doesn't swing at a pitch inside the strike zone, or fouls with less than two strikes

Strikeout – when a batter gets out on three strikes

Sweet spot – the part of the bat that can launch the ball the farthest distance

Tag – when a fielder puts out a runner by touching his body or the ball to the base, or by touching the ball to the runner, before the runner arrives at the base

Take – to let a pitch go by without swinging

Tools of ignorance – the catcher's equipment: protective mask and helmet, chest protector, throat protector, and shin guards

Umpire or Ump – an official who enforces the rules of the game

Underhand – thrown with the hand lower than the belt

Walk – when a hitter gets four balls or is hit by a pitch, which entitles the hitter to a free trip to first base

World Series – a best-of-seven-game series played at the end of the regular major-league baseball season between the champions of the American League and National League

INDEX

• • • • • • • • • • • • • • • • • • • •

Answer to "Try This" page 13: A heated ball can fly farther than a frozen ball—so better to bat with the heated ball and pitch with the frozen ball.